James McNair's
POTATO
COOKBOOK

Photography by Patricia Brabant
Chronicle Books • San Francisco

Printed in Japan.

Library of Congress
Cataloging-in-Publication Data
McNair, James K.
[Potato cookbook]
James McNair's Potato Cookbook
/James McNair;
Photography by Patricia Brabant.
p. cm.
Includes index.
ISBN 0-87701-650-X
ISBN 0-87701-640-2 (pbk.)
1. Cookery (Potatoes) I. Title.
II. Title: Potato cookbook.
TX803.P8M29 1989
641.6'521—dc20   89-17380
                         CIP

Distributed in Canada by
Raincoast Books
112 East Third Avenue
Vancouver, British Columbia V5T 1C8

10 9 8 7 6 5 4 3 2

Chronicle Books
275 Fifth Street
San Francisco, California 94103

For Christine Conn, who's been a second mother, an adopted aunt, and a good friend all rolled into one.

Produced by The Rockpile Press, San Francisco and Lake Tahoe

Art direction, photographic and food styling, and book design by James McNair

Editorial production assistance by Lin Cotton

Food-styling assistance by Ellen Quan

Photography assistance by M. J. Murphy

Typography and mechanical production by Cleve Gallat and Don Kruse of CTA Graphics

CONTENTS

A World-Class Vegetable

INTRODUCTION

The potato is by far the most important vegetable crop in the world. It also ranks as the fourth most important food plant, falling behind only rice, wheat, and corn. But such popularity was not always the case in many places where potatoes are now so beloved.

Searching for gold and silver in 1534, Spanish explorers led by Pizarro "discovered" potatoes cultivated by the Incas some eight thousand feet up in the Andes. The tuber was the staple starch of a civilization that stretched more than two thousand miles, from what is now Ecuador to Chile.

Our word for the vegetable derives from both *batata*, the Spanish pronunciation for the Incan *pappa*, and *patata*, the term the Indians of the American tropics used for the sweet potato. The common names for these botanically distinct plants became the same due to a long period of confusion between the two tubers.

When European sailors returned home with potatoes, enthusiastic gardeners planted them for their ornamental foliage, and the vines quickly spread all the way to Russia. People were skeptical about the tuber itself, however, and for a long time thought it to be poisonous, like its family member, the deadly nightshade.

A few potatoes made their way from Caribbean ports to the Virginia colonies, probably via the ships of Sir Francis Drake in 1586. But the plants went virtually unnoticed. Although other potatoes made their way to American colonial gardens by way of Europe in the early eighteenth century, it was nearly a hundred years before the humble root became a culinary mainstay on either side of the Atlantic.

The Irish were the first since the Incas to cultivate the potato extensively, and to this day many people still refer to the tubers as "Irish potatoes." Unfortunately, the Irish relied almost exclusively on potatoes for their diet, until the tragic blight of 1845-46. A rapidly spreading fungus rotted the tubers, creating a devastating famine during which two and a half million people died. Many Irish who survived this disaster immigrated to the United States, greatly altering the population and political makeup of their new country.

French cuisine, more than any other on earth, has glorified the humble potato. But it took the dedicated efforts and massive publicity campaign of Antoine-Auguste Parmentier, a military pharmacist who learned to enjoy potatoes during his years in a German prison camp, to persuade the French that the ugly tuber was indeed fine food. To this day, numerous potato preparations bear the name Parmentier.

Today France falls closely behind Belgium in annual per capita consumption of potatoes. The average Belgian indulges in 440 pounds per year, or considerably more than a pound a day; the French citizen eats some 420 pounds per year. The market in the United States, where potatoes lead all other vegetables in sales, exceeds $4.5 billion each year, with per capita consumption hovering around 120 pounds, about half of which is eaten in processed form.

The U.S. potato picture also includes the sales and consumption of sweet potatoes, the tropical Latin American native that is botanically unrelated to the white, or Irish, potato. Sold year-round by almost every produce vendor coast to coast, sweet potatoes even outsell their white counterparts in the Deep South. Interest in the sweet, yellow-to-orange fibrous roots is not limited to southern cooks. Sweet potatoes have long been important in the cooking of the Southwest and in country kitchens coast to coast; they now appear on trendy restaurant menus from Manhattan to Seattle. As with white potatoes, Spanish sailors spread sweet potatoes in all directions, north to the American colonies, home to Europe, and across the Pacific to the Philippines, from where they were introduced to the rest of Asia.

This book is filled with updated recipes for potato and sweet potato classics, as well as my own innovations. In some dishes, such as deep-fried chips or soups, the two species are interchangeable; other times sweet potatoes lack the starch needed to bind a dish together. It is my hope that you will discover new ways to enjoy both of these nutrition-packed and extremely satisfying vegetables.

BOTANICALLY SPEAKING

Potato and sweet potato plants produce similar-looking handsome foliage bearing white to purple flowers. There the relationship ends.

Potatoes are edible tubers produced along the fibrous root system of perennial members of the nightshade family (*Solanaceae*), whose relatives include tomatoes and eggplants. Over four hundred species are classified, but only a few are grown commercially.

The sweet potato (*Ipomoea batata*), a tropical American member of the morning-glory family, has varieties whose skin color ranges from reddish brown to pinkish; the flesh of the edible root may be deep orange to yellowish white. The varieties mysteriously misnamed and sold as Louisiana yams tend to be sweeter and moister than other family members. They are not related to true yams, tropical members of the *Dioscorea* family that are only occasionally found in specialty markets outside the tropics.

Types

NUTRITION

According to the United States Department of Agriculture, survival is possible on a diet of potatoes and whole milk.

For far too long potatoes have been maligned as fattening. In fact, one cooked, fiber-rich, medium-sized potato (about 5 ounces), minus any butter or other added fat, contains a mere 110 calories; a half-pounder has only about 160 calories, mostly in the form of complex carbohydrates, along with about 3.2 grams of protein. A single 5-ounce potato supplies about half of the total daily requirement of vitamin C, an abundance of vitamin B_6 (pyridoxine), and beneficial amounts of niacin, pantothenic acid, riboflavin, and thiamin. When you enjoy a potato, you're also helping replenish the body with essential copper, iron, magnesium, potassium, phosphorus, and zinc. Potatoes contain only a trace of sodium.

A comparable serving of plain, cooked sweet potato comes in just under 150 calories and contains a bit less protein than white potatoes. The plus column includes a very large amount of vitamin A and higher doses of calcium, iron, niacin, and potassium.

Although there are over four hundred cataloged species of "white" or "Irish" potatoes, they can be grouped into four categories. Within each group even potato experts may have trouble distinguishing one variety from another. While most potato varieties have white flesh, some produce yellow, purple, or bluish pulp; these offbeat potatoes are becoming more readily available commercially, especially in natural-foods stores and upscale markets.

RUSSETS. The common oblong baking potato, with netted reddish brown skin, is known as the Idaho potato no matter where it is grown, because that state leads in national production. Mature russets cook up floury or mealy, desirable qualities for baking, frying, light dumplings, fluffy mashed potatoes, or other dishes where potatoes do not need to retain their shape. Varieties include 'Russet Burbank' and 'Butte.'

LONG WHITES. These elliptical, somewhat flat-sided potatoes are frequently called California long whites, because they are primarily grown in the Golden State and in Arizona. They have fawn-colored thin skin and almost invisible eyes and are best for boiling and steaming. Varieties include 'White Rose,' 'Kennebec,' and 'Sebago.'

ROUND WHITES. Spherical with smooth, creamy buff skin, these low-starch potatoes are frequently labeled "boiling" or "new potatoes." Varieties include 'Katahdin' and 'Superior.'

ROUND REDS. Smooth, dark red skin covers these round to oblong potatoes, often sold as "boiling" or "new." Varieties include 'Red LaSoda,' 'Red Pontiac,' and 'Viking.'

New potatoes are not a special variety, but any potato harvested before it reaches maturity. The low-starch content precludes long storage, so they must be used quickly. Flesh is moist and waxy, making them good candidates for boiling, steaming, creamy mashed potatoes, and salads. True new potatoes are marketed from late winter or early spring through midsummer.

Many potato recipes use two rather confusing terms — waxy and floury — when specifying potato type. These terms refer to the texture of the potato after cooking, which is dependent on the starch content.

Waxy potatoes are low in starch and high in water content. They keep their shape when cooked, making them ideal candidates for boiling, steaming, simmering, or panfrying or for use in gratins or salads. Choose waxy types if you like creamy, smooth mashed potatoes.

Floury potatoes, sometimes described as mealy, are high in starch and low in water. These fully mature, so-called main-crop potatoes are harvested in late summer or fall when all their sugar has been converted into starch. The flesh becomes loose when cooked, making them best for baking, deep-frying, or mashing when you want a light, fluffy mass.

The trend among American potato growers has been to develop all-purpose potatoes, with a medium range of starch and water. Thus we find very few varieties in today's supermarkets. I've never seen labels reading "waxy potatoes" or "floury potatoes," even though published recipes continue to use these terms. To simplify matters I've used the most common supermarket labels, specifying *baking* potatoes (usually russets) when the floury type is preferred, and *boiling* potatoes when a waxy tuber is desirable. Boiling, or thin-skinned, varieties are often labeled "new" even though they may be quite large and mature. In some recipes the type of potato makes little difference and I have specified the use of either baking or boiling potatoes.

SWEET POTATOES. These irregularly shaped, oblong roots can be divided into two groups: those with dry, pale flesh, less starch, and a subtly sweet flavor such as 'Jersey Gold,' 'Nugget,' and 'Red Garnet' varieties; and the moist, deeper-hued, starchier, and sweeter-tasting varieties sold as "yams." Varieties of the latter include 'Centennial,' 'Gold Rush,' and 'Porto Rico.' Although I usually suggest the yam varieties because of personal preference, either group may be used in recipes that call for sweet potatoes.

Steamed and baked potatoes retain more of their nutrients than potatoes cooked in water. Since the skins are rich in nutrients, it is best to cook potatoes unpeeled or to pare as lightly as possible.

Added fat in the form of butter or sour cream on baked potatoes, oil used for fries, and mayonnaise on potato salad immediately alters the nutritional profile. A single tablespoon of butter doubles the calories in a medium-sized baked potato and frying increases the calorie count by about 350 percent.

Growing

GROWING SWEET POTATOES

Since sweet potatoes are tropical plants, most varieties grow only in areas with a gardening season that runs five frost-free months. Garden catalogs do list a few fast-maturing varieties that can be planted in cooler climates. Sweet potatoes do not grow successfully from cut sections, so you must purchase slips or sprouts.

Plant slips in rich sandy soil with plenty of room for the vines to trail. Avoid overwatering and use low-nitrogen fertilizer sparingly. Expect to harvest early-maturing sweet potatoes in about four months, most varieties in about five months; be sure all are gathered before the first frost. Unless you plan to cook them immediately upon harvest, spread the sweet potatoes out in a dark, very humid, warm (about 85° F) area. After a week transfer them to an indoor storage area as described on the opposite page.

Growing potatoes at home is easy and offers an opportunity to sample many more varieties than are available in markets. Perhaps the best reward are the tasty, tiny new potatoes you can dig as soon as flowers appear on the plants.

Potato plants may be started from seeds or, preferably, from small, whole seed potatoes or cut sections containing three eyes. Certified healthy seed potatoes are available in nurseries or from seed catalogs.

Potatoes from the supermarket probably won't grow because of chemicals used to discourage sprouting. Those from some reliable natural-foods stores may not have been treated and could be satisfactorily planted.

For best results when planting cut sections, dip the cut surfaces into garden sulphur (available from garden centers) to prevent fungus invasions. Place the dipped pieces in full sun until the cuts heal over and calluses form, from two to three weeks.

In the early spring, plant the tuber sections, cut side up, about three inches deep in a well-worked, lightly fertilized sunny spot with good drainage. Water the plants very well about once a week. Expect to harvest a few new potatoes in about two months, when the plants are vigorously growing; be very careful not to disturb roots when digging up the little tubers. Mature tubers are ready for harvesting when most of the plant has died down in late summer or early fall.

To condition potatoes for winter storage, spread them out in a dark, humid location at around 70° F for about a week, then transfer to a storage area as described on the opposite page.

Storing

I was recently amused by a sign over the potato bin in a natural-foods store. It cautioned customers that the world was full of a lot of ugly sights that the eyes of potatoes were never meant to see. This witty warning reinforces the fact that potatoes must be stored in the dark to ward off the development of the glycosidal alkaloid called solanin, which turns the tuber flesh green and is toxic when eaten in quantity. Studies also show that potatoes should not be stored with onions, to avoid the exchange of gases that are detrimental to them both.

The potato storage area should be cool (45 to 50° F), ventilated to prevent sprouting, and humid but not wet; refrigerators are too cold, converting the starch to sugar. Since it's true that one rotten apple, or potato, spoils the whole lot, select only unblemished, perfect potatoes for storage. Any potato will last only about a week at room temperature. Properly stored new potatoes or mature, thin-skinned waxy potatoes keep for only two weeks; baking or mature potatoes or sweet potatoes keep for up to six months. When storing sweet potatoes or thin-skinned potatoes, handle carefully to avoid bruising. Sprouting potatoes may be eaten as long as the potatoes themselves remain firm; remove sprouts before cooking.

Raw potatoes become watery when stored in home freezers; commercial producers of frozen potatoes have special equipment to do the job.

When tightly covered and refrigerated, cooked potatoes last up to three days and cooked sweet potatoes can be kept up to a week. Mashed or puréed cooked potatoes or sweet potatoes can be successfully frozen for up to two or three months.

BUYING

Select potatoes of uniform size if they are to be used for the same dish. They should be firm, fairly smooth, and evenly shaped to prevent waste when peeling. Avoid new potatoes with discolored areas or with sections of their characteristic thin skin rubbed away from rough handling.

For baking, deep-frying, and most all-purpose potato cookery, select dusty-looking mature potatoes. Pass over those with bruises, cuts, or sprouts, as well as any that are shriveled, cracked, soft, hard, or have a green cast.

When buying sweet potatoes, select specimens that are firm all over and without soft spots, cuts, blemishes, or sprouts.

Preparing

YIELDS

Although precise measurements vary according to the moisture content of the potatoes, the following general guidelines may be helpful.

1 pound raw potatoes yields about 2 cups cooked and mashed, or fried.

1 pound raw potatoes yields about 3 cups peeled and sliced, or 2¼ cups peeled and diced.

Average number of raw potatoes per pound:
New potatoes — 14 small, 8 medium;
Mature baking potatoes — 4 small, 1½ large;
Mature thin-skinned potatoes — 5 medium-sized, 3 large;
Sweet potatoes — 2 small, 1 large.

Allow 1 medium-sized or large baking potato per serving.

Depending on size, allow 2 to 4 new potatoes, or about 6 baby potatoes per serving.

If potatoes or sweet potatoes are to be cooked whole in their skins, wash well under running cold water, scrubbing gently with a vegetable brush or cellulose sponge to remove all traces of soil. Remove eyes before cooking.

When peeling potatoes, cut out eyes, sprouts, or discolored spots. Should there be any green areas, trim away this toxic portion; the white part is safe to eat.

Peeled potatoes should be rinsed under running cold water, blotted dry with paper toweling to remove surface starch, and cooked immediately. Recipes that rely on the surface starch to hold slices together eliminate the rinsing step.

Before the advent of rapid transportation, potatoes were stored for longer periods than they are now. This caused them to become quite dry, and many older cookbooks advise lengthy soaking of potatoes in cold water to add moisture, a practice still advocated today by some food writers. Since soaking robs potatoes of nutrients and does not add significantly to moisture content or to the crispness of French fries, I do not recommend this procedure. If you can't cook them right after peeling or slicing, rinse potatoes in a solution of water and a little lemon juice or powdered ascorbic acid to prevent darkening, then drain well and pat dry.

Cooking

I've divided the recipes in this book into three major categories, according to cooking method.

Boiling, Simmering, & Steaming (pages 15-39). This section includes recipes for soups, salads, several dishes with new potatoes, as well as complete directions for the American classic mashed potatoes.

Sautéing & Frying (pages 41-57). In spite of the additional fat that comes from frying, who can resist an occasional heap of French fries? Here are instructions for perfect frying that will add as little fat to the cooked potatoes as possible.

Baking & Roasting (pages 59-93). Perfect baked potatoes are a hallmark of good cooking, so I've included detailed instructions and numerous variations for toppings and stuffings. You'll also find moist potato bread, garlicky roasted potatoes, and several special recipes for sweet potatoes.

Microwave ovens are wonderful time-savers and cook some things as well or better than conventional ovens. Although microwaves certainly speed up the time it takes to bake potatoes, and some people use their ovens almost exclusively for this purpose, I do not recommend them. Too often microwaves render potatoes with gummy centers and uneven texture, and they always produce soft skins. If you don't want to heat up a large oven for one or two potatoes, counter-top toaster ovens do a better job than microwaves.

EQUIPMENT

Potato cookery paraphernalia ranges from expensive copper pans for *pommes Anna* to inexpensive metal prongs for holding baking potatoes, but very little special equipment is needed.

VEGETABLE PEELER. A swivel blade attached to a handle is the best tool for peeling potatoes.

POTATO SLICER. High-priced metal mandolines are great, but a plastic version is okay as long as it has an adjustable blade for varying the thickness of slices.

RICER. Indispensable for mashing. Cooked potatoes are pushed through holes in one direction to form tiny pellets. Unlike a food mill, a ricer does not break up too many starch-filled cells.

DEEP-FAT THERMOMETER. If you deep-fry potatoes and do not own an electric fryer with built-in thermostat, a good thermometer is essential to determine proper temperature for fat.

FRY BASKET. Unless you have an electric fryer that comes with its own basket, choose a wire basket that fits into a large, deep-sided pan.

BOILED & STEAMED

Potato-and-Onion-Family Soup

2 tablespoons unsalted butter
1½ cups chopped white onion
1¼ cups chopped leek, white part
    only (about 4 medium-sized)
½ cup chopped shallots
2 tablespoons coarsely chopped garlic
1 pound boiling or baking potatoes,
    peeled and sliced
Several fresh chervil, parsley,
    marjoram, and/or savory sprigs,
    tied into a bouquet garni
1 quart flavorful homemade vegetable,
    veal, or chicken stock or canned
    chicken broth
1 cup heavy (whipping) cream, light
    cream, or half-and-half
Salt
Freshly ground white pepper
Whole or minced fresh chives
    for garnish

Though many cooks prefer to use only leeks in this French-inspired soup, I've added other members of the onion family for a more complex flavor. Served warm it's hearty fare. Presented chilled, this creamy potato soup goes by the fancy American moniker vichyssoise. A garnish of pesticide-free edible flowers, such as viola, allium, borage, lavender, or other herb blossoms, adds color to the cold soup.

Purple-fleshed Peruvian potatoes create a pale lilac variation; 'Yukon Gold' or other varieties with yellow flesh render a butter-hued soup. For a pale green version, add the leek tops and a handful of minced fresh herbs instead of the bouquet garni. Sweet potatoes also create an unusual variation; swirl a dollop of crème fraîche or whipped sour cream into the hot soup or chill and garnish with slivered orange zest and mint leaves.

In a saucepan, melt the butter over medium heat. Add the onion, leek, and shallots and sauté until soft but not browned, about 5 minutes. Stir in the garlic and sauté 1 minute longer. Add the potato slices, bouquet garni, and stock or broth. Bring to a boil, cover, reduce the heat to low, and simmer until the potatoes are very soft, about 30 minutes. Discard the bouquet garni.

Transfer to a food processor or blender and purée until very smooth. Stir in the cream and season to taste with salt and white pepper. If serving warm, return to a clean saucepan and place over medium heat until hot; do not allow soup to come to a boil. Garnish with chives.

If serving cold, cool completely, cover, and chill for at least 2 hours or as long as 2 days. Just before serving, whisk to blend well, then adjust seasonings, if necessary. Garnish just before serving.

Serves 4 to 6.

North African Potato Soup

If you prefer a smooth version of this exotic porridge, transfer it to a food processor or blender and purée; reheat before serving.

In a stockpot, heat the oil over medium heat. Add the onion and sauté until soft, about 5 minutes. Add the sweet pepper, cumin, and coriander and sauté about 5 minutes. Stir in the garlic, reduce the heat to medium-low, and cook, stirring occasionally, until the onion is almost caramelized, about 35 minutes.

Add the potato slices, tomatoes, stock or broth, and lemon zest and juice. Bring to a boil over medium-high heat, cover, reduce the heat to low, and simmer until the potatoes are tender, about 30 minutes. Stir in salt and peppers to taste. Just before serving, stir in the chopped mint or cilantro. Sprinkle with lemon zest to taste, garnish with mint or cilantro sprigs, and serve hot.

Serves 4 to 6.

¼ cup safflower or other high-quality vegetable oil
2 cups coarsely chopped yellow onion
2 cups chopped red, green, or gold sweet pepper
1 tablespoon ground cumin
2 teaspoons ground coriander
1 entire head garlic, coarsely chopped
2 pounds boiling or baking potatoes or sweet potatoes, peeled and sliced
3 cups peeled, seeded, and chopped ripe tomatoes, or 1 can (28 ounces) crushed Italian plum tomatoes, including juice
1 quart homemade chicken stock, canned chicken broth, or flavorful homemade vegetable stock
1 tablespoon freshly grated lemon zest
2 tablespoons freshly squeezed lemon juice
Salt
Freshly ground black pepper
Ground cayenne pepper
3 tablespoons chopped fresh mint or cilantro (coriander)
Freshly minced lemon zest for garnish
Fresh mint or cilantro (coriander) sprigs for garnish

Potato-Buttermilk Soup

This Eastern European-style soup is guaranteed to warm you up on a cold day. Choose potatoes that will hold their shape after cooking. Serve with good crusty bread.

Place cubed potatoes in a saucepan, add chicken stock or broth to cover barely, and cook over medium heat until the potatoes are tender but still hold their shape, about 10 minutes. Remove from heat but do not drain.

In a skillet, cook the bacon pieces until crisp. Using a slotted spoon, remove the bacon to paper toweling to drain. Add the shallots or onion to the bacon fat and sauté until golden, about 10 minutes. Remove with a slotted spoon and reserve in a small bowl.

Melt the butter in a saucepan over medium-high heat. Add the flour and cook, stirring constantly, for 2 minutes. Slowly stir in the buttermilk and cook until the mixture almost comes to a boil. Stir in the reserved onion, potatoes and their liquid, and minced thyme; heat until the soup comes almost to a boil. Season to taste with salt and pepper.

Ladle into bowls and garnish with the reserved bacon and thyme sprigs.

Serves 4 to 6.

1½ pounds boiling potatoes, peeled and cut into ½-inch cubes
About 2 cups homemade chicken stock or canned chicken broth
6 slices bacon, cut into small dice
1 cup chopped shallots or yellow onion
1 tablespoon unsalted butter
1 tablespoon all-purpose flour, preferably unbleached
5 cups buttermilk
1 tablespoon minced fresh thyme
Salt
Freshly ground white or black pepper
Whole fresh thyme sprigs for garnish

Boiled or Steamed New Potatoes

Perfectly boiled new potatoes are a seasonal joy when tossed with melted butter and topped with a twist or two from the pepper mill. Minced mild herbs add a refreshing flavor and perky appearance; mint is exceptionally good with the earliest spring potatoes.

If desired, pare away a strip of the peel to reveal a band of potato pulp around the middle. This is especially attractive when combining white, yellow, and purple varieties.

Wash the potatoes under running cold water, scrubbing well to remove all traces of soil. Place them in a saucepan, add cold water to cover by about 2 inches, and remove the potatoes. Bring the water to a boil over medium-high heat, add the potatoes, and cook until tender when pierced with a wooden skewer or small, sharp knife, about 10 minutes for tiny potatoes or about 15 to 20 minutes for larger ones. Drain, return the potatoes to the pot, and set over the heat. Shake the pan until moisture evaporates and potatoes are dry to the touch.

Alternatively, place the potatoes on a steamer rack over boiling water, cover, and cook until tender. The times will be slightly longer than those for boiling. Transfer cooked potatoes to a pan, set over heat, and dry as directed above.

Transfer the potatoes to a heated bowl and toss with the melted butter. Sprinkle with herbs and pass the salt and the pepper mill at the table.

Serves 6.

VARIATION: For *pommes anglaise*, cook mature potatoes whole, then cut into halves or quarters and dress as directed. Or cut raw potatoes into quarters or trim them into rounds, oblongs, or cubes and cook as in the recipe.

2 pounds small new potatoes, preferably no more than 1 inch in diameter
6 tablespoons unsalted butter, melted
Minced fresh chervil, mint, or parsley for garnish
Salt
Freshly ground black pepper

Creamed Potatoes

2 pounds boiling potatoes, preferably
    small new potatoes
¼ cup (½ stick) unsalted butter
3 tablespoons all-purpose flour,
    preferably unbleached
2 cups low-fat milk
Salt
Freshly ground white pepper
Minced fresh chervil, mint, or parsley
Whole fresh chervil, mint, or parsley
    sprigs for garnish (optional)

Fancy menus of some years ago quite predictably featured creamed potatoes: peeled, boiled potatoes, usually turned or trimmed into balls or ovals, blanketed with a white sauce. Maybe it's time to resurrect this rich dish once again.

Contemporary dietary concerns have forced a change in this classic, however. Here you will find a light cream sauce made with low-fat milk that tastes like it contains far more calories than it actually does. A richer sauce can be made by using cream or half-and-half.

Wash small whole potatoes under running cold water, scrubbing well to remove all traces of soil. Scrub larger potatoes if you plan to cook them whole (they will be quartered or sliced after cooking). Or peel large potatoes, then turn or trim with a small, sharp knife into perfect ovals, balls, cubes, or other interesting shapes of uniform size.

Cook and dry the potatoes as directed on page 23.

Meanwhile, to make the cream sauce, melt the butter in a saucepan over medium-high heat. Blend in the flour and cook, stirring constantly, for 3 minutes. Slowly add the milk, stirring briskly with a wire whisk or wooden spoon. Reduce the heat so the mixture simmers and continue to cook, stirring or whisking, until the sauce is smooth and thickened. Season to taste with salt and pepper.

Transfer the cooked potatoes to a heated bowl. Pour the sauce over the potatoes and toss to coat. Sprinkle with minced herb and garnish with herb sprigs, if using. Pass the salt and the pepper mill at the table.

Serves 6.

VARIATION: To turn creamed potatoes into the popular Delmonico potatoes, slice the potatoes after boiling, fold them into the white sauce, sprinkle with a little grated Cheddar or Gruyère cheese, if desired, and glaze under a preheated broiler.

New-Potato Salad
in Red Onion Dressing

2 pounds small new potatoes
Salt
Freshly ground black pepper
¾ cup homemade or high-quality
    commercial mayonnaise
¾ cup sour cream or plain yogurt
½ cup finely chopped sweet red onion
½ cup minced fresh dill or parsley,
    preferably flat-leaf type
Fresh dill or parsley sprigs for garnish

This simple potato salad is exceptionally good with summer barbecue. It is also delicious tossed with a whole-grain-mustard vinaigrette instead of the mayonnaise dressing.

Wash the potatoes under running cold water, scrubbing well to remove all traces of soil.

Cook and dry the potatoes as directed on page 23. Transfer the potatoes to a bowl and cut into halves, quarters, or slices, if desired. Season to taste with salt and pepper. Cool slightly before dressing.

In a bowl, combine the mayonnaise, sour cream or yogurt, onion, and dill or parsley and blend well. Pour over the warm potatoes and toss gently to mix thoroughly. Garnish with herb sprigs and serve at room temperature or slightly chilled.

Serves 6.

VARIATIONS: Cook only 1 pound potatoes. Combine with 1½ cups cooked, shelled fresh green peas. Substitute ¼ cup minced fresh chives or green onion for the red onion and ½ cup chopped fresh mint for the dill or parsley.

For the old-favorite potato-and-green-bean combo, separately cook 1 pound potatoes and 1 pound green beans. Toss together with either the red-onion mayonnaise or a mustard vinaigrette.

Potato and Mussel Salad (*Salade Francillon*)

BASIL VINAIGRETTE
¾ cup fruity olive oil, preferably
    extra-virgin
¼ cup white wine vinegar
¼ cup dry white wine
3 tablespoons chopped fresh basil
Salt
Freshly ground black pepper

2 pounds medium-sized boiling
    potatoes
24 fresh mussels in the shell, bearded
    and scrubbed, then steamed in
    2 inches of fish stock or dry white
    wine until opened
Fresh young salad greens such as
    dandelion, mâche, or arugula,
    washed, dried, and chilled
Cherry tomatoes
Niçoise olives
Minced fresh or preserved black
    truffle (optional)
Pesticide-free edible flowers such as
    nasturtium or scented geranium
    for garnish (optional)
Fresh basil sprigs for garnish

The original version of this updated salad, based on a recipe repeated by a character in the younger Alexandre Dumas's *Francillon*, showed up on the menus of fashionable Parisian restaurants soon after the play's premiere.

The success of this salad depends on firm potato slices, so start with waxy boiling potatoes.

To make the vinaigrette, combine the oil, vinegar, wine, basil, and salt and pepper to taste and blend well; reserve.

Wash the potatoes under running cold water, scrubbing well to remove all traces of soil. Place in a saucepan and add water to cover by 2 inches, then remove the potatoes. Bring the water to a boil over medium-high heat, add the potatoes, and cook until just tender when pierced with a wooden skewer or small, sharp knife, about 25 to 30 minutes; avoid overcooking. Drain, return the potatoes to the pan over heat, and shake the pan until excess moisture evaporates and potatoes are dry to the touch.

When cool enough to handle, peel potatoes and cut crosswise into ⅜-inch-wide pieces. If desired, carefully trim with a scallop-edged cookie cutter. While still warm, gently toss with about half of the vinaigrette. Cool to room temperature.

Alternatively, peel the scrubbed potatoes, slice and trim with the cookie cutter, and steam in a rack over boiling water until just tender. Dress as for boiled potatoes.

Remove the mussels from their shells, toss with about half of the remaining vinaigrette, and cool to room temperature.

To assemble, line each of 4 individual plates with greens. Add a circle of potato slices, overlapping slices slightly. Arrange 6 mussels in the center of each plate and add tomatoes, olives, and minced truffle (if used). Drizzle with remaining vinaigrette to taste. Garnish with flowers (if used) and basil. Serve at room temperature.

Serves 4.

All-American Potato Salad

This picnic classic is hard to beat. It can be varied in numerous ways according to individual tastes and what is on hand—chopped or minced olives, celery, sweet pepper, green onion, fresh herbs.

Wash the potatoes under running cold water, scrubbing well to remove all traces of soil. Place them in a saucepan and add water to cover by about 2 inches, then remove the potatoes. Bring the water to a boil over medium-high heat, add the potatoes, and cook until just tender when pierced with a wooden skewer or small sharp knife, about 25 to 30 minutes. Drain, return the potatoes to the pan over heat, and shake the pan until excess moisture evaporates and potatoes are dry to the touch.

As soon as the potatoes are cool enough to handle, peel them, cut into cubes or slices of uniform size, and place in a large bowl.

In a separate bowl, whisk or stir together the mayonnaise, mustard, and lemon juice or vinegar. Gently toss enough of the dressing into the warm potatoes to coat completely. Stir in the eggs, chopped sweet pepper, onion, pickle, parsley, and salt and pepper to taste.

Serve the salad at room temperature or slightly chilled. Just before serving, garnish with crumbled bacon and sweet pepper.

Serves 6.

VARIATION: For mashed potato salad, press the peeled, cooked potatoes through a ricer. While still warm, add the dressing and continue as above.

2 pounds boiling potatoes
1 cup homemade or high-quality commercial mayonnaise
1 tablespoon Dijon-style mustard
2 tablespoons freshly squeezed lemon juice or white wine vinegar, or to taste
3 hard-cooked eggs, chopped
½ cup finely chopped red sweet pepper
½ cup minced white or yellow onion
½ cup finely chopped bread-and-butter pickles or sweet pickle relish
3 tablespoons minced fresh parsley
Salt
Freshly ground black pepper
Crisp fried bacon, crumbled, for garnish
Red or gold sweet pepper, cut into decorative shapes, for garnish (optional)

Mashed Potatoes

While the homey mashed potato has recently skyrocketed to gourmet status, some food writers have waxed nostalgically about the characteristic lumps. Those who equate mashed potatoes with lumps were living with lazy cooks who didn't take the time or use the right technique to remove the lumps.

Take your choice as to the type of potato to use: boiling or waxy potatoes whip up smooth and creamy; baking potatoes produce a fluffy dish. In either case, avoid using potato mashers or food mills, which break up too many starch-filled cells and cause stickiness. And never subject potatoes to electric beaters or food processors; they'll whip them into glue.

For ways to dress up the potatoes, look to the suggestions on pages 34-35.

Wash the potatoes under running cold water, scrubbing well to remove all traces of soil. Place them in a saucepan and add water to cover by about 4 inches, then remove potatoes. Alternatively, peel the potatoes, cut into pieces of uniform size about ¾ inch thick, and rinse under cold running water to remove surface starch. Place them in a saucepan and add water to cover by 2 inches, then remove potatoes.

In either case, bring the water to a boil over medium-high heat, add the potatoes, and cook until just tender when pierced with a wooden skewer or small, sharp knife, about 35 to 45 minutes for whole potatoes, or about 15 to 20 minutes for slices; avoid overcooking. Drain, return the potatoes to the pan over heat, and shake the pan until excess moisture evaporates and potatoes are dry to the touch. As soon as whole potatoes are cool enough to handle, peel and cut into chunks.

Press hot potatoes through a ricer into a large bowl. Stir in the melted butter, ½ cup heated cream, and salt and pepper to taste. Using a wooden spoon or wire whisk, whip the potatoes until light and fluffy, adding additional warm cream if required to form desired consistency; avoid making the potatoes too thin. Serve immediately or keep warm in a partially covered container set over warm (not simmering) water.

Makes about 4 cups, serves 4 to 6.

2 pounds potatoes (see recipe introduction for type)
¾ cup (1½ sticks) unsalted butter, melted
About ½ cup heavy (whipping) cream, heated
Salt
Freshly ground white pepper

MASHED POTATO VARIATIONS

ALTERNATE COOKING METHOD FOR MASHED POTATOES

This rather unorthodox method of cooking potatoes in two stages with a cold-water resting bath in between results from suggestions made by instant-mashed-potato-industry experts. It produces mashed potatoes that are a bit lighter than those prepared by the orthodox method.

Peel the potatoes, cut into pieces of uniform size about ¾ inch thick, and rinse under cold running water to remove surface starch.

Place potatoes in a saucepan, add water to cover the potatoes by 2 inches, and remove the potatoes. Insert a kitchen thermometer into the water and heat to 175° F. Add the potatoes, adjust the heat to maintain a temperature of about 160° F, not quite a simmer, and heat for about 25 minutes. Drain the potatoes and transfer to a bowl. Cover with cold water and let stand until the potatoes are cold, about 35 minutes.

Drop the partially cooked potatoes into a saucepan of boiling water or arrange in a steamer rack over simmering water and cook until the potatoes are just tender when pierced with a wooden skewer or small, sharp knife; avoid overcooking, which releases too much starch. Drain the potatoes and continue as directed on page 33.

Prepare the potatoes as directed on the preceding page, adding one of the following suggestions.

Combine the riced potatoes with an equal portion of puréed cooked beet, carrot, cauliflower, celeriac (celery root), green bean, lima bean, parsnip, rutabaga, mushroom, or turnip before adding butter and cream.

When adding the heated cream, mix in a combination of minced fresh herbs such as chives, parsley, sage, savory, or tarragon.

Mound the whipped potatoes on an ovenproof platter or in a shallow bowl and generously sprinkle the top with freshly grated Parmesan cheese, shredded Gruyère, or other good-melting cheese. Place in a preheated 400° F oven until the cheese melts.

Sprinkle finished whipped potatoes with toasted dried bread crumbs or chopped nuts, minced fresh herbs, chopped pitted black olives, or a dusting of ground paprika or cayenne pepper.

CLASSICS

Croquettes de pommes de terre. Omit the cream. Beat in 2 or 3 eggs with the butter, then spread potatoes in a shallow dish and let stand until cold. Shape into rounds, flat-topped pyramids, or patties. Dip into beaten egg and then into fine fresh bread crumbs; deep-fry in high-quality vegetable oil until golden brown. Minced ham, truffle, olive, or herbs, tomato purée, or other seasonings may be added to taste to the whipped mixture.

Himmel und Erde. For this German classic, which translates as "heaven and earth," peel, core, and quarter 2 pounds tart apples. Place in a saucepan and cook over low heat with 1 tablespoon granulated sugar and 2 teaspoons freshly grated lemon zest until soft. Mash the apples and whip them with the buttered riced potatoes, substituting chicken stock or broth for the cream. Fry 4 thick bacon slices in a skillet until crisp; remove with a slotted utensil to drain on paper toweling, then crumble. Sauté 2 large onions, sliced, in the bacon drippings until translucent. Stir the onion and crumbled bacon into the potato-apple mixture. The dish is traditionally topped with slices of cooked blood sausage.

Pommes de terre à la biarritz. Add about ¾ cup finely diced baked ham, ½ cup sautéed green sweet pepper, and ¼ cup minced fresh parsley when whipping the potatoes.

Pommes de terre à la chantilly. Spread the whipped potatoes in a buttered flameproof dish. Whip ½ cup heavy (whipping) cream until stiff but not grainy, spread it over the potatoes, and place under a preheated broiler until the top is lightly browned.

Pommes de terre à la nostiz. Prepare the croquette mixture (preceding). Shape into square flat cakes, dip in melted butter, and then in freshly grated Parmesan cheese. Arrange on a buttered baking sheet, sprinkle with fine fresh bread crumbs, drizzle with crawfish-flavored butter, and bake until golden.

Pommes de terre duchesse. Omit the cream. Beat in 1 whole egg and 2 egg yolks with the butter and season with freshly grated nutmeg to taste. For a decorative border around roasted meats or baked whole fish, transfer the mixture to a pastry bag fitted with a large, decorative tip. Pipe the potatoes in a wide fluted band, or form rosettes or other decorations around the edge of an ovenproof serving platter holding the meat or fish. Remove the meat or fish, brush potatoes with melted unsalted butter, and bake until golden brown in a preheated 400° F oven. Return the meat or fish to the platter and serve.

To cook as a garnish, spread the egg-enriched whipped potatoes in a shallow dish and let stand until cold. Roll pieces of the potato mixture into small cylinders and panfry in hot oil until golden brown. Drain briefly on paper toweling before serving. Or pipe the mixture into rosettes or other fancy shapes on a buttered baking sheet; brush all over with melted butter and brown in a preheated 400° F oven.

Pommes de terre mousseline. Omit the cream. Beat in 4 egg yolks with the butter. Whip ½ cup whipping (heavy) cream until stiff but not grainy; fold cream into potatoes. Mound in an ovenproof dish, drizzle with melted butter, and bake in a preheated 450° F oven until golden brown.

REDUCING FAT AND CALORIES

Obviously my mashed potato recipe is not a low-fat dish, even though I use little butter in comparison to some French recipes that call for as much as 1 pound of butter for every 2 pounds of potatoes.

It's also possible to get by with a bit less butter than I suggest; adjust the recipe to fit your dietary restrictions. Polyunsaturated margarine, if you can accept the flavor, certainly cuts the saturated fat, though not the calories. Olive oil, used alone or in combination with butter, adds a fruity flavor for a change of pace without adding saturated fat.

The liquid reserved from boiling the potatoes, flavorful stock or broth, half-and-half, low-fat buttermilk, or even low-fat milk can be used instead of the cream for a less-rich dish.

Italian-Style Potato Dumplings (*Gnocchi di Patate*)

2 pounds large boiling potatoes
About 1½ cups all-purpose flour,
    preferably unbleached
Salt
4 quarts water
¼ cup (½ stick) unsalted butter,
    melted
1½ cups freshly grated Parmesan
    cheese, preferably Parmigiano-
    Reggiano
Minced fresh thyme, basil, or other
    fresh herb (optional)

Toss *gnocchi* with melted butter and cheese as directed in the recipe, or select a favorite fresh tomato, marinara, mushroom, pesto, or Bolognese meat sauce for mixing with the dumplings. You may also toss the gnocchi with butter and cheese and then serve it on a pool of the selected sauce as shown here.

Cook, dry, and peel the potatoes as directed on page 33.

Push the hot peeled, cooked potatoes through a ricer into a large bowl. Add 1 cup of the flour and about 1 teaspoon salt, or to taste. Knead with fingers until smooth, adding more flour a little at a time until the dough is no longer sticky. Form the mixture into a loaf.

In a large pot, bring the water to a boil over high heat. Add about 1 tablespoon salt, if desired.

Meanwhile, cut off a lengthwise piece of the dough about 1½ inches thick. On a lightly floured surface, roll the dough with your palms into a rope about ¾ inch thick. Cut into 1¼-inch lengths. Dust fingertips with flour and press and roll each piece of the dough against the inside of a flour-dipped fork so that one side has the impression of the tines and the other has a dent in the middle made by your finger; or roll the middle of each piece against the work surface with a finger to form a bow shape. It is important that the centers be about the same thickness as the outer areas, so that the dumplings cook evenly. Repeat this process with the remaining dough.

As soon as all the dough is shaped, drop about 12 dumplings at a time into the boiling water. After they rise to the surface, continue to cook about 10 to 15 seconds, then remove with a slotted utensil to a heated bowl and toss in a little of the melted butter or some of the sauce (see recipe introduction). Cover the container with aluminum foil to keep the contents warm while you cook the remaining gnocchi, adding each batch to the bowl as they are done.

Just before serving, toss the gnocchi with the remaining butter or sauce and about ⅔ cup of the Parmesan cheese. Pass additional cheese at the table.

Serves 6.

Guatemalan Potato Tamales
(*Paches con Papas*)

This unusual recipe was given to me by Victoria Flores and is a specialty of her homeland. It requires pork lard for authentic flavor. Surprisingly, perhaps, lard has only half the saturated fat of butter.

Heat a skillet over medium heat, place the split chilies in it, and toast until dry and fragrant, about 2 minutes; do not burn. Transfer to a spice grinder or food processor and grind until powdery; reserve. If using chili powder, reserve.

Boil the potatoes as directed on page 33, using pork broth or fresh or canned chicken broth instead of water; drain, reserving liquid, and dry as directed. Mash, but eliminate butter and use reserved liquid in place of cream.

Heat about 3 tablespoons of the lard in a sauté pan or skillet over medium-high heat. Add the onion and sweet pepper and sauté until soft, about 5 minutes. Add the garlic, tomatoes, oregano, and reserved ground chilies or chili powder to taste and cook until the vegetables are very tender, about 20 minutes. Season to taste with salt and pepper. Transfer to a large bowl, stir in the mashed potatoes and shredded or chopped pork.

Heat the remaining 3 tablespoons lard in the sauté pan or skillet over medium-high heat. Add the potato mixture and sauté, breaking up the mixture with a wooden spoon, to heat through and combine flavors.

Shake excess water from the corn husks. Spread out large single pieces or overlap two smaller ones. Spoon about ½ cup of the potato mixture into the center of the wrapper and bring the sides up and over the filling so that they overlap. Tie ends of each packet with strips torn from extra husks; the ends should flare out. Chill overnight.

Place the tamales on a steamer rack set over boiling water and steam until heated through, about 30 to 45 minutes. Serve immediately.

Makes about 12 tamales, serves 6 to 8.

3 or 4 dried *pasilla* chili peppers, washed, split, and seeded, or about 3 tablespoons high-quality chili powder
2 pounds boiling potatoes
About 1 quart homemade pork or chicken stock or canned chicken broth
6 tablespoons high-quality rendered pork lard (in Spanish, *manteca*; available in Mexican markets) or high-quality vegetable oil
1½ cups finely chopped yellow onion
1 cup finely chopped green or red sweet pepper
1 tablespoon minced or pressed garlic, or to taste
2 cups peeled, seeded, and chopped ripe tomatoes or drained, canned Italian plum tomatoes
2 teaspoons crumbled dried oregano
Salt
Freshly ground black pepper
2 cups shredded or chopped, cooked boneless pork shoulder
About 30 single sheets dried corn husk wrappers (available in Mexican food shops and some supermarkets), covered in water until softened, about 30 minutes

SAUTÉED & FRIED

Sautéed Stuffed Potato Slices

2 pounds boiling or large new
    potatoes
1 egg, beaten
Fresh herb leaves such as basil,
    cilantro (coriander), flat-leaf
    parsley, or sage
About ½ cup (1 stick) unsalted butter,
    clarified (see note)
Salt
Freshly ground black pepper

Arrange these attractive herb-filled potato "sandwiches" alongside grilled, poached, or sautéed fillets of fish, poultry, or meat. Or serve on a bed of greens as an unusual salad.

Instead of herb leaves, fill the potato slices with dollops of finely minced sautéed mushrooms, fresh black truffle slices, or garlicky herbed cheese.

Cut the potatoes as thinly as possible, using a mandoline or other slicing device. Trim slices into a fancy shape with a cookie cutter. Do not rinse and dry (all the starch is needed to ensure the slices hold together).

Lay out half of the potato slices on a flat surface and brush lightly with beaten egg. Place an herb leaf on each slice, then cover with a second slice, pressing well to seal the slices together. Cover and chill for about 30 minutes.

In a sauté pan or skillet (preferably with a nonstick surface) over medium heat, melt enough butter to coat the bottom of the pan. Without crowding, add the potato slices, a few at a time, and cook, shaking the pan frequently and carefully turning the sandwiches once, until the potatoes are tender and just beginning to turn golden. Add more butter to the pan as needed to keep the potatoes from sticking. Remove to paper toweling to drain briefly. Season to taste with salt and pepper. Keep warm in a preheated 200° F oven until all are cooked. Serve hot.

Serves 6 to 8.

NOTE: To clarify butter, melt it in a small saucepan over low heat. Remove from the heat and let cool for a few minutes; the milk solids will settle to the bottom of the pan. Skim the butterfat from the top and strain the clear (clarified) butter into a container; discard the milk solids. Keeps indefinitely in the refrigerator.

Potato Pancakes

Crisp, thin pancakes made from grated potatoes are usually eaten as a side dish with roast beef or chicken, often with a dollop of applesauce. For breakfast, top with a poached or fried egg.

1 pound baking potatoes
3 eggs, lightly beaten
⅓ cup grated chopped yellow onion
3 tablespoons all-purpose flour, preferably unbleached
2 tablespoons light cream or half-and-half
Salt
Freshly ground black pepper
About ¾ cup (1½ sticks) unsalted butter or high-quality vegetable oil for panfrying

Peel and coarsely grate the potatoes. Place in a cloth towel or heavy-duty paper toweling and squeeze to remove as much moisture as possible.

Beat the eggs in a large bowl. Add the potatoes, onion, flour, light cream or half-and-half, and salt and pepper to taste and stir to blend thoroughly. Cover and chill for 1 hour.

In a sauté pan or skillet, melt enough butter or pour in enough oil to cover the bottom of the pan. Heat over medium-high heat until hot but not smoking. Without crowding the pan, drop in about 3 tablespoons of the potato mixture per pancake and flatten with the back of the spoon to form fairly thin, even cakes. Cook until golden brown on one side, then turn and cook until the other side is golden and the edges are crispy, about 5 minutes total cooking time. Transfer to a preheated 200° F oven to keep warm until all pancakes are cooked. Serve hot.

Serves 4.

VARIATIONS: Substitute grated carrot, celeriac (celery root), parsnip, or other root crop for half of the potatoes.

For pancakes with an Asian accent, omit the grated onion; add to potato mixture, ½ cup finely chopped green onion, ¼ cup toasted sesame seeds, 2 teaspoons minced or pressed garlic, 2 tablespoons minced fresh cilantro (coriander), and 2 tablespoons soy sauce. Cook in vegetable oil and sprinkle with sesame seeds and minced fresh cilantro.

For Jewish *latkes*, cook the pancakes in rendered chicken fat; for Passover, substitute matzo meal for the flour.

Potato Cakes with Peanut Sauce (*Llapingachos con Salsa de Maní*)

POTATO CAKES
2 pounds boiling or baking potatoes
3 tablespoons lard, unsalted butter,
    or peanut or other high-quality
    vegetable oil
2 cups finely chopped yellow onion
3 eggs, lightly beaten
⅔ cup all-purpose flour, preferably
    unbleached
2 cups (about 6 ounces) freshly
    shredded Emmenthaler, Gruyère,
    Monterey jack, or sharp white
    Cheddar cheese
¼ cup (½ stick) unsalted butter,
    melted
Salt
Freshly ground black pepper

PEANUT SAUCE
2 tablespoons lard, unsalted butter,
    or peanut or other high-quality
    vegetable oil
1 tablespoon *achiote* (annatto seeds;
    available in Mexican markets)
1 cup finely chopped yellow onion
2 teaspoons minced or pressed garlic,
    or to taste
2 cups peeled, seeded, and chopped
    ripe tomatoes or canned Italian
    plum tomatoes, including juice
1 cup unsalted dry-roasted peanuts,
    finely ground
Salt
Lard, unsalted butter, or peanut or
    other high-quality vegetable oil
    for panfrying
Pitted black olives, cut into decorative
    shapes, for garnish

Variations on these panfried potato cakes are popular throughout Colombia, Ecuador, and Peru, where potatoes have been a staple since pre-Incan times. The time-honored peanut sauce accompaniment is sensational.

To make the potato cakes, scrub, boil, dry, peel, and rice the potatoes into a bowl as directed on page 33. Do not add other ingredients as directed in that recipe.

Heat the lard, butter, or oil in a sauté pan or skillet over medium-high heat. Add the onion and sauté until soft and golden, about 8 to 10 minutes. Pour over the potatoes. Add the eggs, flour, cheese, melted butter, and salt and pepper to taste and beat with a wooden spoon or wire whisk to blend well. Divide the mixture into 12 pieces. Roll each piece into a ball, then flatten into a cake on a baking sheet or platter. Cover and refrigerate the cakes until well chilled, at least 2 hours or as long as overnight.

To make the peanut sauce, heat the lard, butter, or oil in a sauté pan or skillet over medium heat. Add the *achiote* and heat just until the fat turns deep orange, about 1 minute; remove from heat and strain and discard the seeds. Return pan with achiote-flavored fat to medium-high heat, add the onion, and sauté until soft, about 5 minutes. Add the garlic and sauté 1 minute longer. Stir in the tomatoes, reduce the heat to medium-low, and cook about 5 minutes. Add the peanuts and cook, stirring constantly, until heated through, about 3 minutes. Transfer to a food processor or blender and purée until well blended. Season to taste with salt. Keep warm or reheat before serving.

To cook the potato cakes, add enough lard, butter, or oil to coat the bottom of a sauté pan or skillet. Without crowding, fry the cakes, a few at a time, until golden brown on the bottom. Turn and fry until golden brown on the other side, about 5 minutes total cooking time. Drain briefly on paper toweling and keep warm in a preheated 200° F oven until all cakes are cooked. Garnish with olives and serve with the warm peanut sauce.

Serves 6.

Open-Faced Potato Omelet

Similar dishes are known in Spain as _tortilla española_ and in Italy as _frittata con le patatine_.

Serve wedges as a light lunch or supper dish, or cut into bite-sized pieces for tapas.

Peel the potatoes and slice thinly or cut into tiny cubes. Rinse in cold water and pat dry with paper toweling. Season to taste with salt and pepper.

In a large sauté pan or skillet (preferably with a nonstick surface), combine the vegetable and olive oils over medium-high heat. Add the potatoes and cook, turning occasionally, until lightly golden, about 8 minutes; do not expect potatoes to hold their shape. Add additional oil as needed to keep potatoes from sticking. Using a slotted utensil, transfer the potatoes to paper toweling to drain.

Add the onion to the same oil used to cook the potatoes and sauté over low heat until soft and golden, about 25 minutes. About halfway through cooking, add the sweet pepper. Using a slotted utensil, drain the onion-pepper mixture as well as possible and reserve in a bowl. Clean the pan with paper toweling.

In a large bowl, beat the eggs lightly. Stir in the reserved potato, onion-pepper mixture, parsley, and salt and pepper to taste.

In the same pan over medium heat, melt the butter until foamy. Pour in the egg mixture and spread evenly. Turn the heat to low and cook until the omelet is set except for the top, about 10 to 15 minutes. Cover with a plate slightly larger than the skillet and invert the omelet onto it. Slide the omelet back into the skillet and cook until the eggs on the bottom are set, about 3 to 5 minutes longer. Alternatively, do not invert the omelet onto a plate; place the skillet under a preheated broiler until the top is just set but not browned, about 1 minute. Loosen the omelet with a spatula and slide onto a serving platter. Garnish with red pepper curls and serve warm.

Serves 4 to 6.

2 pounds boiling or baking potatoes
Salt
Freshly ground black pepper
¼ cup safflower or other high-quality vegetable oil
About ¼ cup fruity olive oil, preferably extra-virgin
2 cups thinly sliced yellow onion
½ cup minced red sweet pepper
6 eggs
¼ cup minced fresh parsley
3 tablespoons unsalted butter
Thin red sweet pepper strips, soaked in iced water until curled, for garnish

Swiss-Style Straw Mat Potatoes (*Rösti*)

Similar to America's famous panfried potato cakes combine a crunchy crust with a meltingly tender interior. Butter is the traditional cooking fat for flavorful potatoes, but cholesterol watchers may choose to substitute polyunsaturated oil or margarine.

To garnish the plate as shown, smear a bit of softened butter or vegetable oil on the plate rim wherever you want the minced parsley to adhere. Sprinkle with parsley and brush away any that falls in spaces between the greased areas. Add the potato cake and sprinkle the top with more parsley to continue the design from the plate rim.

Sometimes a sprinkling of grated Gruyère, Emmenthaler, or other Swiss cheese is scattered over the top of the potatoes after they are flipped. By the time the bottom is crusty, the cheese will have melted.

Peel the potatoes and shred them about ⅛ inch thick. Do not rinse; just pat natural moisture dry with paper toweling. Season to taste with salt and pepper.

Melt 4 tablespoons of the butter in a skillet over medium heat. Add the drained potatoes and cook until the bottom is golden brown and crusty, about 5 minutes; shake the pan occasionally to prevent the potatoes from sticking. Reduce the heat and cook about 5 minutes longer to cook the interior partially. Cover the skillet with a flat plate, invert the pan, and turn the potatoes onto the plate. Increase the heat again and melt the remaining 4 tablespoons butter. Slip the potato cake back into the skillet. Cook, shaking the pan frequently, until the bottom is crusty, about 5 minutes, then reduce the heat and cook until the interior is tender, about 5 minutes longer.

Slide the cake onto the serving plate, garnish with the parsley, and serve immediately.

Serves 4.

2 pounds baking potatoes
Salt
Freshly ground black pepper
½ cup (1 stick) unsalted butter,
    clarified (see note, page 42)
Minced fresh parsley for garnish

Spiced Potato Balls (*Aloo Vada*) with Cilantro-Coconut Chutney

CILANTRO-COCONUT CHUTNEY

2 bunches fresh cilantro (coriander), bottom stalks discarded and tops coarsely chopped

8 fresh green serrano or other small hot chili peppers

¼ cup freshly squeezed lemon juice

½ cup grated fresh or unsweetened dried coconut

About 2 tablespoons granulated sugar

About 1 teaspoon salt

SPICED POTATO BALLS

1 tablespoon safflower or other high-quality vegetable oil

½ teaspoon mustard seeds, preferably black

Pinch ground asafetida (optional)

1 cup minced yellow onion

2 tablespoons minced fresh green serrano or other hot chili peppers

2 pounds boiling potatoes, cooked and riced (page 33)

½ cup chopped fresh cilantro (coriander)

1 teaspoon ground turmeric

Salt

Ground cayenne pepper

2 cups garbanzo (chick-pea) flour (about 8 ounces)

1 teaspoon *garam masala* spice mix

¼ teaspoon baking soda

Safflower or other high-quality vegetable oil for deep-frying

Mariam Sodergren showed me how to prepare this fiery appetizer, which is good with traditional mango, tamarind, or other sweet chutney in addition or as an alternative to the cilantro one given here. Any unfamiliar ingredients are available from East Indian grocers or some natural-foods stores.

To make the chutney, combine the cilantro, chilies, and lemon juice in a food processor or blender and process until well chopped. Add coconut and sugar and salt to taste and purée, adding a little water if necessary to form a thick paste. Cover and refrigerate (lasts up to 5 days).

To make the potato balls, heat the oil in a saucepan over medium-low heat. Add the mustard seeds and asafetida, if using, cover, and cook until the seeds stop popping, about 45 seconds. Remove cover, increase the heat to medium-high, add the onion and chilies, and cook until the onion is soft. Add the mashed potatoes, cilantro, turmeric, and salt and cayenne pepper to taste; cook until ingredients are heated through and well blended. Remove from heat and cool to room temperature. Break off pieces of the potato mixture about the size of an unshelled walnut and roll into balls between palms of hands. Chill on a tray until fairly firm, about 30 minutes.

In a bowl, combine the garbanzo flour, *garam masala*, baking soda, ¼ teaspoon salt, and ½ teaspoon cayenne pepper. Add enough water to make a batter about the consistency of pancake batter.

Pour the oil into a deep-fat fryer or deep pan to a depth of about 2 inches. Heat until temperature reaches 375° F on a deep-fat thermometer.

Working with a few balls at a time, dip the cold potato balls into the batter, then carefully drop into the hot fat; do not use a fry basket as the batter sticks to the wire. Cook, turning frequently, until golden brown, about 5 minutes. Remove to paper toweling to drain. Serve immediately, with the chutney for dipping, or keep warm in a preheated 200° F oven until all the balls are fried.

Serves 8 to 10 as a starter.

Fried Potatoes
(*Pommes de Terre Frites*)

Baking potatoes (allow 1 medium-
sized potato per person)
Safflower, peanut, or other high-
quality vegetable oil or solid
vegetable shortening for deep
frying

Deep-fried potatoes will be crispier when fried twice, in the French manner, though very thin cuts can be cooked successfully at higher heat in only one frying. Potatoes can be cut into a wide variety of shapes for deep frying. A few suggestions are shown in the photograph and described on the following pages.

An electric deep-fat fryer with built-in thermostat makes potato frying a breeze, but a deep pot, a long-handled wire basket, and a deep-fat thermometer work just fine.

Don't forget that sweet potatoes, especially yam varieties, also make unusually scrumptious fries; thin cuts work best.

Peel the potatoes and cut into desired shape (see pages 56-57 for suggestions). Be sure all pieces are about the same size. Rinse in cold water and pat completely dry with paper toweling. Or spin in a salad spinner, then finish drying with paper toweling.

Meanwhile, pour the oil into a deep-fat fryer or deep pan to a depth of about 2 inches. Place over medium heat until temperature reaches 325° F.

Transfer the dried potatoes to a fry basket and slowly immerse the basket into the hot fat. Alternatively, carefully drop by handfuls into the hot fat; avoid overcrowding. Cook until the potatoes are cooked and soft but not beginning to turn golden, about 3 minutes for thin cuts to about 5 minutes for thick cuts. Remove from the fat, transfer to paper toweling, and let drain for at least 5 minutes or up to several hours.

Shortly before serving, heat the cooking fat to 375 to 395° F. Return the potatoes to the hot fat and fry until crisp and golden, about 3 minutes for straw cuts to about 5 minutes for thick cuts. Drain briefly on paper toweling to remove surface grease, then serve hot. (If cooking a lot of potatoes, transfer each batch to a preheated 200° F oven until all are cooked.)

One medium-sized potato makes 1 serving.

SUGGESTED CUTS FOR FRIED POTATOES

BATTER-FRIED POTATOES

My first taste of batter-coated French fries was at The Fish Fin, a rustic restaurant specializing in fantastic fried catfish out in a swamp near my hometown of Jonesville, Louisiana. I always return to enjoy these fries when I visit my parents.

Following directions for Fried Potatoes, peel potatoes, cut into traditional French-fry sticks, rinse in cold water, and dry well. Dip sticks into beaten egg blended with a drizzle of milk, then into flour seasoned with salt (or into fine dried bread crumbs or fine cornmeal); shake off excess coating. Deep-fry only once in peanut oil preheated to 375° F until golden.

Balls. Form spheres with a melon-ball scoop; save scraps for soup.

Chips (American) or Crisps (British). Slice crosswise into desired thickness, from paper-thin to about ⅛ inch.

Crinkles. Slice on a special ripple-bladed cutter into French-fry-sized pieces.

Cubes. Trim into perfect cubes of desired size.

Nests or Baskets. Cut as for straw potatoes (following) or as for thin chips. Dip a set of overlapping wire baskets with a long handle (sold in cookware stores) into hot fat, then arrange straws or rounds inside the larger basket, cover with the smaller basket, and lower into the hot oil until the potatoes are crisp. Carefully remove each potato nest to paper toweling to drain. Keep warm in a preheated 200° F oven until all nests are fried. Fill with sautéed or stir-fried vegetables, purées (page 83), or stews or other saucy meat dishes.

Puffed (*Soufflé*). Use large baking potatoes that have been stored for 2 to 3 months or until skin cannot be penetrated with a fingernail. Slice lengthwise ⅛ inch thick, preferably with a slicing machine. Trim edges of each slice to form a wide football shape, making all pieces the same size. Slices *must* be absolutely dry before the first cooking. Stir the potatoes with a wooden spoon or shake the basket during both the first and second fryings to agitate the fat. Depending upon the potato, most slices will puff up during the second frying; since all will not puff perfectly, start with about twice as many as you plan to serve. Unpuffed slices are just as tasty but lack the drama.

Scallops (*Collerettes*). Slice crosswise about ⅛ inch thick, then cut with a scalloped cookie cutter; remove center with a small round or scalloped cutter.

Shavings (*Chatouillard* or *Copeaux*). Use a rotating vegetable peeler and cut in a continuous spiral to create thin ribbons as long as possible and about ½ inch wide.

Shoestring (*Cordon de Soulier*) or Straw (*Paille*). Cut lengthwise into julienne about as thick as matchsticks; leave shoestrings as long as possible, cut straw into 3-inch lengths.

Sticks, French Fries (American), or Chips (British). Slice lengthwise into sticks about 3 inches long and from ¼ to ½ inch thick.

Waffles. Use a mandoline cutter or other slicer to cut thinly crosswise, then rotate a quarter turn before the next cut. Leave round or trim into squares.

POTATO SKINS

Cut baked potatoes lengthwise into strips about 1 inch wide, leaving about ⅜ inch of the potato pulp attached; reserve remaining pulp for another purpose. (Or save tops cut from baked potatoes that will be stuffed; they can be accumulated in self-sealing plastic bags and frozen for several months.) Deep-fry in high-quality vegetable oil preheated to 375° F until crisp.

If desired, top fried potato skins with shredded cheese, chopped green onion, minced mild or hot canned chili peppers, crumbled crisp bacon, or other favorite topping. Place under a preheated broiler until the cheese melts.

For a less caloric version, do not deep-fry. Spread the potato skin strips on a baking sheet and bake in a preheated 450° F oven until crisp. Add toppings and broil to melt cheese.

Baked & Roasted

Baked Potatoes

A perfectly baked potato is a hallmark of good cooking. Choose potatoes with unblemished skin and with flesh that is white and dry. Once baked, the nutrient-laden edible skin should be crisp and the interior soft and dry. Rubbing with butter or oil results in soft skin. Forget foil wrapping, too; it produces insipid steamed potatoes with limp skin. Although time-savers, microwaves turn out a baked potato with unappealing texture and soft skin.

Potatoes adapt to a range of oven temperatures and cooking times, so they can be baked in the oven when it is already in use for other dishes. At 350° F, they will cook in about 1 hour and 20 minutes; at 450° F, the potatoes should be done in about 45 minutes.

Offer potatoes with one or more of the suggested toppings, such as the three caviars, minced chives, and sour cream shown here accompanied by a glass of chili pepper vodka.

See page 81 for directions for baking sweet potatoes.

Preheat an oven to 375° F.

Wash potatoes under running cold water, scrubbing well to remove all traces of soil. Dry with paper toweling and prick in several places with the tines of a fork.

Place potatoes directly on an oven rack and cook until the flesh gives and feels soft when squeezed through a clean kitchen towel between thumb and fingers, about 1 hour.

Split the potatoes and press all around with fingertips to loosen the pulp. Add a dollop of butter and serve piping hot. Season to taste with salt and pepper at the table. Offer one or more of the suggested toppings for diners to add as desired.

Each potato makes 1 serving.

Large baking potatoes (allow
   1 per person)
Softened unsalted butter
Salt
Freshly ground black pepper

OPTIONAL TOPPINGS
Sour cream, crème fraîche, or
   plain yogurt
Compound butter (softened unsalted
   butter blended with minced
   herbs, garlic, or other seasonings)
Minced fresh chives or green onions
Minced fresh herbs such as basil,
   marjoram, oregano, savory,
   or thyme
Shredded Cheddar, fontina,
   Monterey jack, or other
   good-melting cheese
Freshly grated Parmesan cheese
Crumbled chèvre (goat's milk cheese)
   or blue cheese
Crumbled crisply fried bacon
Crumbled sun-dried tomatoes
Sautéed chopped onion and garlic
Chopped olives
Minced fresh or preserved truffles
Black, red, or golden caviar

Stuffed Baked Potatoes

4 large baking potatoes
¼ cup (½ stick) unsalted butter,
    melted
6 ounces cream cheese, softened
½ cup sour cream or crème fraîche
½ cup freshly grated Parmesan cheese,
    preferably Parmigiano-Reggiano
½ cup minced fresh chives, marjoram,
    oregano, parsley, sage, or other
    herbs (or a combination)
Salt
Freshly ground black pepper
Additional melted butter for
    brushing tops

Twice-baked potatoes filled with a wide range of stuffings have become popular everywhere. Many combinations sold in take-away potato stands are quite awful, though some are very tasty. This recipe explains the basic technique and gives directions for a creamy rich stuffing. The next two pages include a few classics of haute cuisine, as well as some innovations to serve as guidelines for creating your own house specialties. Baked sweet potatoes (page 81) can be scooped and blended with orange juice or zest, chopped fresh mint, ginger, or other compatible seasonings, then stuffed and rebaked.

Scrub and bake the potatoes as directed on page 61.

Cutting lengthwise, slice off the top 1 to 1½ inches from each potato (if desired, reserve in freezer bag for Potato Skins, page 57). Alternatively, slice very large potatoes in half lengthwise to make 2 servings. In either case, carefully scoop the pulp into a warmed bowl, leaving about a 1/8-inch shell all around and being careful not to tear the skin. Reserve the shells.

Preheat an oven to 400° F or a broiler.

Press the warm pulp through a potato ricer into a large bowl. Add the melted butter, cream cheese, sour cream or crème fraîche, grated cheese, minced herbs, and salt and pepper to taste. Beat with a wooden spoon or wire whisk until light and fluffy. Scoop the mixture into the reserved skin shells, mounding slightly, and create a decorative pattern on top with a dull knife blade or spatula. Alternatively, transfer the potato stuffing to a pastry bag fitted with a large, decorative tip and pipe into the shells for a fancier presentation.

Place the potatoes in a baking dish or on a baking sheet. Brush the tops with melted butter and place in oven or under a broiler until the tops begin to turn golden brown, about 10 to 15 minutes in the oven, or about 4 to 5 minutes in a broiler.

Serves 4.

POTATO STUFFING VARIATIONS

LOW-CALORIE STUFFING SUGGESTIONS

Add 2 cups stir-fried or steamed mixed vegetables to the riced potato pulp. Thin the mixture with low-fat milk, if necessary. Brush tops of stuffed potatoes with a little olive oil before baking. Garnish with fresh minced herbs.

Beat about 1 cup small-curd cottage cheese and ¼ cup minced fresh herbs into the riced pulp and season to taste with freshly squeezed lemon juice. Lightly sprinkle stuffed potatoes with freshly grated Parmesan cheese before baking.

Blend 2 cups puréed cooked beet, carrot, celeriac (celery root), or turnip with the riced potato pulp, thin with low-fat milk, and season to taste. Brush tops of stuffed potatoes with a little olive oil before baking.

For each of the following variations, cook, split, and rice 4 large potatoes as directed on page 62. Add a little heavy (whipping) cream, light cream, half-and-half, or milk to any of the following fillings if it seems dry.

FRENCH CLASSICS

Pommes de terre à l'ardennaise. Combine the riced pulp with ¼ cup melted unsalted butter, 1 cup finely chopped, cooked chicken breast, ½ cup finely chopped baked ham, ½ cup minced fresh chives, and salt and freshly ground white pepper to taste. Beat until fluffy, stuff into shells, and sprinkle with about ½ cup freshly shredded Gruyère cheese. Bake in a preheated 400° F oven until the cheese is bubbly, about 5 to 10 minutes. Garnish with whole chives and serve immediately.

Pommes de terre à la bohémienne. Combine the riced pulp with 2 cups crumbled cooked pork sausage and salt and freshly ground black pepper to taste. Beat until fluffy, stuff into shells, and brush the tops with melted unsalted butter. Bake in a preheated 400° F oven until tops are golden, about 5 to 10 minutes. Sprinkle with finely chopped red sweet pepper and serve immediately.

Pommes de terre à la commodore. Combine the riced pulp with ¼ cup melted unsalted butter, 2 cups puréed cooked spinach, ¼ cup minced fresh parsley, 2 tablespoons Worcestershire sauce, or to taste, and freshly grated nutmeg, salt, and freshly ground black pepper to taste. Beat until fluffy, stuff into shells, and brush the tops with melted unsalted butter. Bake in a preheated 400° F oven until tops are golden, about 5 to 10 minutes. Sprinkle with minced fresh parsley and serve immediately.

Pommes de terre farcies à la ménagère. Sauté 1½ cups chopped yellow onion in 3 tablespoons unsalted butter until soft. Combine with the riced pulp, ⅔ cup finely chopped baked ham, ½ cup light cream or half-and-half, and salt and pepper to taste. Beat until fluffy, stuff into shells, sprinkle with about ½ cup freshly shredded Cheddar cheese, and dot with about 3 tablespoons unsalted butter, cut into small pieces. Bake in a preheated 400° F oven until the cheese is bubbly, about 5 to 10 minutes.

Pommes de terre à l'italienne. Combine the riced pulp with 2 cups cooked rice, 1 cup tomato purée, ½ cup freshly grated Parmesan cheese (preferably Parmigiano-Reggiano), ¼ cup chopped fresh basil or 2 tablespoons chopped fresh oregano (or 2 teaspoons crumbled dried oregano), and salt and freshly ground black pepper to taste. Beat until fluffy, stuff into shells, sprinkle with additional Parmesan, and drizzle with fruity olive oil, preferably extra-virgin. Bake in a preheated 400° F oven until the cheese is bubbly, about 5 to 10 minutes. Garnish with fresh basil or oregano sprigs and serve immediately.

OTHER SUGGESTIONS

Garlic Seafood. Sauté ½ cup finely chopped green onion (including tops) in ¼ cup unsalted butter until soft. Add 1 tablespoon minced or pressed garlic and sauté 1 minute longer. Add 2 cups chopped cooked crab, crawfish, lobster, scallops, or shrimp and ¾ cup dry white wine, sherry, or vermouth; cook until the liquid evaporates. Stir in ½ cup heavy (whipping) cream, crème fraîche, or sour cream. Combine with the riced pulp and salt and freshly ground white pepper to taste. Beat until fluffy, stuff into shells, and sprinkle the tops with about ½ cup freshly grated Parmesan cheese. Bake in a preheated 400° F oven until cheese is bubbly, about 5 to 10 minutes. Garnish each serving with additional cooked seafood and fresh tarragon or other herb sprigs and serve immediately.

Southwest Style. Combine the pulp with ½ cup diced canned green mild chili peppers or fiery *chipotle* chili peppers (ripened, smoked jalapeños), ½ cup freshly grated sharp Cheddar cheese, ⅓ cup sour cream, ¼ cup minced fresh cilantro (coriander), and salt and ground cayenne pepper to taste. Beat until fluffy, stuff into shells, and sprinkle with an additional ½ cup grated Cheddar. Bake in a preheated 400° F oven until the cheese melts, about 5 to 10 minutes. Top each potato with dollops of sour cream and guacamole, sprinkle with minced ripe olives, garnish with a sprig of cilantro, and serve immediately.

LUXURIOUS STUFFING SUGGESTIONS

Combine with the riced potato pulp, 1 cup crème fraîche or sour cream and fresh black, red, or golden caviar to taste and budget. After baking, garnish with minced chives, sieved hard-cooked egg yolk, and additional caviar.

Sauté as much fresh truffle as you wish in unsalted butter. Beat into the riced potato pulp. Before baking, sprinkle tops of stuffed potatoes with additional truffle and freshly grated Parmesan cheese and brush with melted unsalted butter.

Sauté 1 tablespoon minced or pressed garlic and 2 tablespoons chopped sun-dried tomatoes in 3 tablespoons unsalted butter. Combine sautéed mixture with the riced potato pulp, 1 cup crumbled chèvre (goat's milk cheese), and ½ cup heavy (whipping) cream, whipped until stiff but not grainy. Brush tops with melted butter. After baking, garnish with garlic blossoms or other flowering herbs.

Sauté 2 to 3 cups finely chopped fresh mushrooms, preferably wild varieties such as *chanterelles, morels, porcini,* or *shiitakes*, in 3 tablespoons unsalted butter. Beat into the riced potato pulp.

Warm Crispy Potato Salad

4 large baking potatoes
About 4 cups small fresh arugula,
    endive, radicchio, sorrel, or
    spinach leaves or other salad
    greens
Fruity olive oil, preferably
    extra-virgin
Balsamic or other red wine vinegar
Salt
Freshly ground black pepper

I once read that potatoes baked for a long time in a very hot oven until quite crisp were a favorite of the late James Beard. True or not, the method attributed to him yields potatoes that are reminiscent of fried potato skins without the extra cooking fat. They make a warm textural counterpoint to the cold crisp greens in this unusual salad.

Preheat an oven to 450° F.

Wash potatoes under running cold water, scrubbing well to remove all traces of soil. Dry with paper toweling and prick in several places with the tines of a fork.

Place potatoes directly on an oven rack and cook until the skin is very crispy, about 2 hours.

Meanwhile, rinse the greens under running cold water, dry thoroughly, wrap in a clean cloth towel, and refrigerate to crisp.

Arrange the chilled greens on 4 individual plates. Slice the hot potatoes in half lengthwise, then cut each section in half lengthwise. Distribute four pieces on top of each plate of greens. Drizzle the potatoes and greens with olive oil and sprinkle with vinegar to taste. Serve immediately. Pass the salt and a pepper mill; pepper should be added generously.

Serves 4.

Dilled Potato Bread

½ pound boiling or baking potatoes
1 package active dry yeast
1 tablespoon granulated sugar
1½ cups warm (110 to 115° F) water
    or liquid from cooking potatoes
1 cup buttermilk
2 tablespoons unsalted butter, melted,
    or high-quality vegetable oil
1 tablespoon salt
¼ cup chopped fresh dill
About 8 cups all-purpose flour,
    preferably unbleached
About ¼ cup pastry flour

Cook and mash the potatoes as directed on page 33; do not add other ingredients. Reserve cooking liquid, if desired.

In a large mixing bowl, gently stir together the yeast, sugar, and warm water or potato cooking water until the yeast dissolves, about 1 minute. Let stand in a warm spot until a thin layer of foam covers the surface, about 5 minutes, indicating that the yeast is effective. (Discard mixture and start over with a fresh package of yeast if bubbles have not formed within 5 minutes.)

Add the warm mashed potato, buttermilk, melted butter or oil, salt, and dill and stir to combine thoroughly. Add 7 cups of the flour and mix well. Turn the dough out onto a lightly floured surface and knead for 2 or 3 minutes, adding as much of the remaining 1 cup flour, a little at a time, as needed until the dough is no longer sticky. Set aside for 10 minutes.

Continue kneading the dough until quite elastic, supple, and smooth. Gather into a ball and place in a greased bowl, turning to coat all over. Cover with plastic wrap and let stand in a warm, draft-free area until doubled in bulk, about 1½ hours.

Punch the dough down and knead it for about 5 minutes. Form the dough into a large round loaf and place in a greased shallow, round pan about 12 inches in diameter, or divide the dough in half, form each portion into a loaf, and place in 2 greased 9-by-5-inch loaf pans. Cover loosely with plastic wrap or waxed paper and let rise for about 30 minutes.

Preheat an oven to 350° F.

Using a sharp knife or kitchen scissors, slash the top of the loaf (or loaves) with crosses, diamonds, or parallel incisions. Lightly mist top(s) with warm water and dust with pastry flour. Bake until nicely browned, about 1 hour or more for the large loaf, about 45 to 50 minutes for the smaller loaves. Turn out onto wire racks to cool for about 15 minutes.

Makes one 12-inch loaf or two 9-by-5-inch loaves.

Roasted Potatoes
with Garlic and Rosemary

2 pounds (about 25) small new
  potatoes
2 tablespoons coarsely chopped garlic
1 tablespoon fresh or dried rosemary
  leaves
½ cup fruity olive oil, preferably
  extra-virgin
Coarse salt
Freshly ground black pepper

This is how I most frequently cook potatoes. They go perfectly with roast lamb, grilled or smoked fish or meats, or melted cheese.

For a simple yet sublime starter, offer a bowl of sour cream, plain yogurt, or homemade mayonnaise for dipping. For fancier appetizers suitable for passing, cut a thin layer from the top of each potato, hollow an indentation with a melon-ball scoop, and fill with a tasty stuffing — dabs of sour cream with smoked salmon or caviar, soft cheese blended with minced sun-dried tomato, or other favorites. Or stuff with a piece of *raclette* cheese and a slice of cornichon and heat in the oven until the cheese melts. Garnish each potato with a tiny sprig of fresh herb.

When purchasing the potatoes, try to find purple or yellow varieties in addition to regular white ones. When small new potatoes aren't available, larger potatoes can be quartered, sliced, or cut into 1-inch cubes.

Preheat an oven to 375° F.

Place the potatoes in a roasting pan or other ovenproof shallow container. Add the garlic, rosemary, olive oil, and salt and pepper to taste. Turn potatoes in the seasonings to coat all sides. Roast, stirring occasionally, until the potatoes are tender when pierced with a wooden skewer, about 35 to 45 minutes.

Serves 6 to 8 as a side dish.

VARIATIONS: Add minced anchovy fillets or crumbled sun-dried tomatoes to the olive oil for a more pronounced Mediterranean flavor.

Potatoes Anna (*Pommes Anna*)

Special large copper pans are used by restaurants to cook this grand dish created in honor of a fashionable French woman named Anna Deslions. Various-sized skillets, shallow round baking dishes, or glass pie plates will work in the home kitchen; just distribute the mixture evenly among the smaller pans. Attractive individual servings can be arranged in tart pans with removable bottoms, baked until the top is golden, then transferred, top side up, with a spatula onto plates.

The potatoes may also be served directly from the baking container when an easier presentation is appropriate.

Peel the potatoes and trim each lengthwise into an even cylinder. Cut crosswise, preferably with a mandoline or other cutting device, into slices about 1/16 inch thick. If desired, trim each slice with a small round biscuit cutter to create a uniform circle. Rinse in cold water and pat dry with paper toweling. Season slices to taste with salt and pepper.

Preheat an oven to 450° F.

Brush about 2 tablespoons of the butter in 2 medium-sized skillets or other shallow, round baking dishes. In each container arrange a layer of potatoes in a spiral design, overlapping each slice. Drizzle a bit more of the butter over the layer. Repeat this step two more times, making 3 layers of potatoes in all.

Bake until the potatoes are tender when pierced with a wooden skewer or small, sharp knife and the bottoms are golden brown, about 45 minutes. Several times during cooking, press the top of the potatoes with a flat instrument to create a compressed cake of even thickness.

Using a spatula, carefully loosen the sides and bottom of the potatoes from the pan, pour off and discard excess butter, and invert the potato "cakes" onto warm serving plates.

Serves 6 to 8.

2½ pounds baking potatoes
Salt
Freshly ground black pepper
¾ cup (1½ sticks) unsalted butter, clarified (page 42) and remelted

Potatoes Gratin

2 pounds potatoes (See page 76 for type)
5 tablespoons unsalted butter
Salt
Freshly ground white pepper
Freshly grated nutmeg
¼ cup minced fresh chives or green onions, including part of green tops
2 teaspoons minced or pressed garlic, or to taste
1 cup light cream or half-and-half combined with ¾ cup heavy (whipping) cream
Whole or minced chives for garnish

Whether you call it by one of its fancy French names — *gratin de pommes à la boulangère, gratin de pommes à la crème, gratin de pommes à la dauphinoise* — or dub it plain old scalloped potatoes, there is no more succulent treatment of potatoes than slices cooked in cream, milk, or stock until meltingly tender. The variations on this classic, each with its own moniker, are endless. This basic recipe is followed by several elaborations on the theme.

Peel the potatoes. Trim sides to form even cylinders or rectangles, if desired. Slice as thinly as possible with a mandoline or other slicing device. Quickly rinse the slices in cold water and pat them dry with paper toweling.

Preheat an oven to 300° F.

Melt 3 tablespoons of the butter and pour into a gratin or other ovenproof serving dish. Using about one third of the potato slices, arrange a single layer in the bottom of the dish. Sprinkle with salt, pepper, and nutmeg to taste and about half of the minced chives or green onion and garlic. Add a second layer of potato slices, using about half of what remains, and top with the seasonings and the remaining chives or green onion and garlic. Top with a final layer of potato slices; the dish should be no more than three-quarters full. Pour the cream mixture over the top to cover the potatoes barely. Cut the remaining 2 tablespoons butter into small pieces and dot the top. Sprinkle with salt and pepper to taste.

Place in the middle rack of the oven and bake until the potatoes are tender, most of the liquid has been absorbed, and the top is lightly browned, about 1½ to 2 hours. If top is not brown, increase the temperature to 375° F during the last 10 minutes of cooking. Serve immediately or keep warm in a 200° oven for up to 1 hour. Garnish with chives.

Serves 4.

GRATIN VARIATIONS

Each of these dishes is based on 2 pounds potatoes cooked in a shallow dish that is 10 to 12 inches in diameter; the ingredients also can be divided among individual gratin dishes. In either case, the potatoes should be peeled and cut as in the preceding recipe and, in all except the American Scalloped Potatoes, arranged in no more than 3 layers. All are baked in a 300° F oven until most of the liquid is absorbed, the potatoes are tender, and the top is lightly browned or the cheese topping is bubbly.

For a quicker-cooking version, cover the sliced potatoes with liquid in a saucepan and simmer until tender on top of the stove, then layer in a shallow, glazed earthenware or porcelain gratin or other oven-to-table baking dish, cover with more liquid, and finish in the oven.

CLASSICS

American Scalloped Potatoes. In a buttered 3-quart baking dish, alternate 4 layers of potatoes, seasoned to taste with salt and freshly ground black pepper, with 4 layers of thinly sliced yellow onion (use 1 large onion). Sprinkle each onion layer with 1 tablespoon all-purpose flour, preferably unbleached, cover with ½ cup freshly shredded Cheddar cheese, and dot with about 2 tablespoons unsalted butter, cut into small pieces. Add just enough milk to cover the ingredients. Cover with a lid or aluminum foil and bake until the liquid is bubbly, about 45 to 55 minutes. Uncover and continue baking until the potatoes are tender and the top is lightly browned, about 30 to 40 minutes.

Gratin de pommes à la boulangère. Thinly slice 2 yellow onions and sauté in 3 tablespoons olive oil until golden brown. In a buttered baking dish, alternate layers of potato slices, seasoned to taste with salt, white pepper, and freshly grated nutmeg, with layers of the onion, ending with potatoes. Add flavorful homemade beef stock or canned beef broth to cover. Combine ¾ cup freshly shredded Gruyère and ½ cup freshly grated Parmesan cheese and sprinkle over the potatoes. Dot with butter and bake.

POTATO TYPE

Choose boiling potatoes that will retain their shape during cooking. If you prefer potato layers that almost melt together instead of remaining distinct, use baking potatoes and do not rinse them after slicing; just pat off the excess natural moisture and the starch will help the layers stick together.

Don't forget sweet potatoes and yam varieties for a gratin of a different hue and flavor.

Gratin de pommes à la dauphinoise. Butter a baking dish and then rub well with cut sides of garlic cloves. Arrange up to 3 layers of potato slices in the dish. Combine 3 beaten eggs, 1 cup milk, and 1 cup heavy (whipping) cream and pour over the potatoes. Sprinkle with a grated mild cheese such as Gruyère and bake.

Gratin de pommes à la savoyard. Alternate 3 layers of thin potato slices in a buttered baking dish with small pieces of unsalted butter and shredded semisoft mild French cheese, such as Pont-l'Evêque or Saint-Nectaire, or Swiss cheese, such as Emmenthaler, in between the layers. Add homemade chicken, beef, or veal stock or canned broth to cover the potatoes and bake.

OTHER VARIATIONS

Sprinkle potato layers with crumbled blue cheese or tangy goat's milk cheese.

Sprinkle potato layers with finely chopped baked ham or slivered prosciutto.

Sprinkle potato layers with minced fresh herbs of choice.

Scatter sautéed wild or domestic mushrooms in between potato layers.

Reduce the amount of potatoes and add a surprise middle layer of thinly sliced carrots or turnips.

Cover the potatoes with cream sauce (page 24) instead of suggested liquid.

Sprinkle top with fresh bread crumbs and dot with butter before baking.

Potato Knishes in Phyllo

¼ cup rendered chicken fat, unsalted butter, or high-quality vegetable oil
1 cup finely chopped yellow onion
2 cups warm riced potatoes (page 33)
2 eggs
Salt
Freshly ground black pepper
1 pound phyllo pastry, thawed in the refrigerator if frozen
About ½ cup (1 stick) unsalted butter, melted

In this unusual treatment of Jewish knishes, flaky phyllo pastry is a crisp counterpoint to the soft potato interior.

Heat the chicken fat, butter, or oil in a sauté pan or skillet over medium-high heat. Add the onion and sauté until soft, about 5 minutes.

In a large bowl, combine the mashed potatoes, sautéed onion, eggs, and salt and pepper to taste. Reserve.

Cut enough phyllo sheets into 5-inch squares to make about 80 pieces. (Leftover phyllo can be used for another purpose. Fresh dough can be frozen for later use; do not refreeze thawed dough.) Place 1 square on the work surface and keep the remaining dough covered with a lightly dampened cloth towel to prevent it from drying out. With a pastry brush, lightly brush the phyllo square with melted butter to cover completely. Top that sheet with a second one and lightly brush it with butter. Repeat until you have stacked 5 sheets. Spoon about 3 tablespoons of the potato mixture into the center of the top sheet. Bring one corner of the phyllo up and over to cover the filling and brush the top of the dough with butter. Fold the remaining phyllo corners up and over the filling, overlapping and buttering them as you go. Place each phyllo package, seam side down, on a greased baking sheet.

Preheat an oven to 350° F.

Brush all exposed phyllo with melted butter and bake the knishes until the phyllo is golden brown, about 20 minutes. Serve immediately or while still warm.

Serves 4 or 5.

VARIATION: Chopped cooked liver or other meat may be added to the basic mixture.

Baked Sweet Potatoes

In some households, sweet potatoes are offered only at Thanksgiving. Around my home, this nutritious tuber is an occasional, very satisfying light meal all on its own and appears frequently as a creamy side dish year-round. I enjoy baked sweet potatoes, usually the sweeter, moister varieties labeled "yams," with a little melted butter and a dusting of powdered sugar or some warm maple syrup for breakfast or a late-supper sweet treat.

Preheat an oven to 400° F.

Wash the sweet potatoes under running cold water, scrubbing well to remove all traces of soil. Dry with paper toweling and prick in several places with the tines of a fork.

Place sweet potatoes directly on an oven rack and cook until the flesh gives and feels soft when squeezed through a clean kitchen towel between thumb and fingers, about 35 to 55 minutes.

Split the sweet potatoes, add a dollop or drizzle of butter, and serve piping hot.

Each potato makes 1 serving.

Sweet potatoes, 12 ounces to 1 pound each (allow 1 per person)
Softened or melted unsalted butter

Sweet Potato and Chestnut Purée

1 pound fresh chestnuts, or 1 cup
   imported canned, unsweetened
   chestnut purée (available
   in gourmet shops and some
   supermarkets)
About 2 cups homemade chicken
   stock, canned chicken broth, or
   water, if using fresh chestnuts
1 pound sweet potatoes (about 1 large),
   preferably varieties labeled yams
½ cup (1 stick) unsalted butter,
   melted
1 cup heavy (whipping) cream, heated
Salt
Freshly ground white pepper

Vegetable purées are one of my favorite side dishes. Offer this smooth, change-of-pace purée as an elegant addition to autumn or winter holiday meals.

For the presentation shown here, deep-fry sliced sweet potatoes in nesting baskets as directed on page 56. Pipe in the purée and serve immediately.

With a small, sharp knife, score an *X* on the flat side of each chestnut. Place the chestnuts in a pan, cover with cold water, and bring to a boil over high heat. Cook for 2 minutes. Drain.

When the chestnuts are cool enough to handle, peel off and discard hard outer shell and inner fine membrane and place in a saucepan. Add enough stock, broth, or water to cover and bring to a boil over medium-high heat. Reduce the heat to low and simmer, uncovered, until tender, about 45 minutes. Drain the chestnuts, reserving the liquid. Transfer the chestnuts to a food processor or blender and purée until smooth, adding a little of the reserved cooking liquid, if necessary, to make a smooth purée; reserve. If using canned purée, reserve.

Scrub and bake the sweet potatoes as directed on page 81. Alternatively, cook, uncovered, in a microwave at high power until tender, about 15 minutes.

When the sweet potatoes are cool enough to handle, peel and cut into chunks. Place in a food processor or blender and purée until fairly smooth. Add the chestnut purée, melted butter, cream, and salt and pepper to taste. Blend until smooth.

Heat to serving temperature in a microwave or in the top pan of a double boiler set over simmering water. Serve warm.

Serves 6 to 8.

Sweet Potato Waffles

1 cup mashed peeled, baked sweet
  potato (about 1/2 pound),
  preferably varieties labeled yams
  (page 81)
½ cup (1 stick) unsalted butter,
  melted
2 eggs, separated
1 cup milk
1 cup sifted all-purpose flour,
  preferably unbleached
2 teaspoons baking powder
½ teaspoon salt, or to taste

Waffles enriched with mashed sweet potatoes and drizzled with warm maple syrup have long been a morning favorite in my kitchen. But waffles needn't be restricted to classic breakfast presentations. The savory combination pictured here is my version of a dish I enjoyed at Arizona 206, a trendy but superb southwestern restaurant in New York City. Grilled turkey breast is sandwiched between two small waffle squares and served with mole sauce.

Preheat a waffle iron.

In a bowl, combine the sweet potato, butter, egg yolks, and milk and beat until blended. Add the flour, baking powder, and salt and stir until smooth.

In a separate bowl, beat the egg whites until stiff but not dry. Fold into the batter mixture. Bake according to directions from your waffle iron manufacturer. Serve hot.

Serves 4.

Pecan-Streusel-Topped Sweet Potatoes

Juanita Cheek, back in Lake Providence, Louisiana, introduced me to this southern casserole, and it has remained a favorite way of preparing sweet potatoes. I occasionally pour the mixture into a partially cooked pastry crust and bake it as a pie.

Scrub and bake the sweet potatoes as directed on page 81. Alternatively, place the sweet potatoes in a pot and add cold water to cover. Bring to a boil over medium-high heat and cook until almost tender, about 35 to 45 minutes. Drain.

Preheat an oven to 350° F.

As soon as the sweet potatoes are cool enough to handle, peel, cut into chunks, and press through a ricer into a bowl; do not use a food processor as it will make them too smooth. Add the eggs, melted butter, and milk or half-and-half and beat until well blended. Pour into a buttered 2-quart baking dish.

In a bowl, combine the softened butter, flour, brown sugar, and pecans and mix well with your fingertips. Sprinkle the mixture evenly over the top of the potatoes. Bake until the topping is bubbly, about 1 hour. Garnish with mint and lavender and serve warm or at room temperature.

Serves 6 to 8.

3 pounds sweet potatoes, preferably varieties labeled yams
2 eggs, beaten
¼ cup (½ stick) unsalted butter, melted
½ cup milk or half-and-half
¼ cup (½ stick) unsalted butter, softened
¼ cup all-purpose flour, preferably unbleached
⅔ cup firmly packed light brown sugar
1 cup chopped pecans
Fresh mint leaves for garnish
Pesticide-free lavender flowers for garnish (optional)

Sweet Potato Kisses

Whether you serve these delicate morsels as a brunch dish, an unusual accompaniment to afternoon tea, alongside roast pork or duck, or as an airy dessert, be sure to pipe and brown them only minutes before serving.

Scrub and bake the sweet potatoes as directed on page 81. As soon as the sweet potatoes are cool enough to handle, peel them and press through a ricer into a bowl. Add the eggs, sugar, salt to taste, and orange juice or liqueur and zest. Using a wooden spoon or wire whisk, beat until smooth and fluffy.

Preheat a broiler.

Transfer the mixture to a pastry bag fitted with a large, fluted tip. Pipe onto orange slices and arrange on a lightly greased baking sheet. Drizzle tops with melted butter and place under the broiler until lightly browned.

Dust with powdered sugar, garnish with blossoms, and serve warm.

Serves 4 to 6.

3 pounds sweet potatoes, preferably varieties labeled yams
4 eggs
¼ cup granulated sugar, or to taste
Salt
2 tablespoons freshly squeezed orange juice or orange-flavored liqueur
1 tablespoon freshly minced or grated orange zest
2 or 3 medium-sized oranges, sliced about ⅛ inch thick
About ¼ cup (½ stick) unsalted butter, melted
Powdered sugar for dusting
Pesticide-free edible flowers such as scented geranium or borage for garnish (optional)

Country French Potato Cake (*Galette de Pomme de Terre*)

2 pounds baking potatoes or
    sweet potatoes
3 egg yolks
⅓ cup unsalted butter, melted
¾ cup granulated sugar
½ teaspoon salt
2 tablespoons freshly minced or
    grated lemon zest
2 tablespoons orange flower water,
    or to taste
1 egg beaten with 2 tablespoons heavy
    (whipping) cream or half-and-half
    for glazing
Crystallized violets, pulverized in
    a food processor or spice grinder,
    or granulated sugar for
    sprinkling
Pesticide-free flowers such as citrus,
    jasmine, lavender, and lilac
    for garnish (optional)

For centuries, numerous types of flat, round French cakes, or *galettes*, have been made from a variety of ingredients. Potatoes are turned into both savory and sweet versions of this peasant tradition.

Scrub and bake the potatoes as directed on page 61, or the sweet potatoes as directed on page 81.

Preheat an oven to 375° F.

As soon as the potatoes are cool enough to handle, peel and press through a ricer into a large bowl. Add the egg yolks, butter, sugar, salt, lemon zest, and orange flower water and beat until smooth and fluffy.

Gather the potato mixture into a ball, then press it flat with your palm. Repeat this process 3 or 4 more times. Flatten it the final time on a buttered baking sheet; shape the mixture into a round cake about 1½ inches thick. Draw a spatula or dull knife blade through the top of the cake to create a design. Brush the top and sides with the egg glaze and sprinkle with pulverized violet or sugar.

Bake until golden brown, about 20 minutes. Transfer to a serving dish, sprinkle with flowers, if using, and serve hot or warm; cut into wedges.

Serves 4 to 6.

SAVORY VARIATION: Do not use sweet potatoes. Omit the sugar, lemon zest, and orange flower water. Add a bit more salt and season to taste with freshly ground white pepper. Use garlic butter in place of unseasoned butter. Omit sprinkling of pulverized violet or sugar and the flower garnish; sprinkle with minced fresh herbs after baking.

Caribbean Sweet Potato-Coconut Loaf (*Gateau de Patate*)

2 pounds sweet potatoes, preferably varieties labeled yams
½ cup mashed ripe banana
1 cup firmly packed light brown sugar
1 teaspoon baking powder
½ teaspoon salt
½ teaspoon ground cinnamon
¼ teaspoon freshly grated nutmeg
4 eggs, well beaten
1 cup milk, preferably evaporated milk
¼ cup (½ stick) unsalted butter, melted
¼ cup dark rum, or 1 teaspoon vanilla extract
1 cup finely shredded fresh or sweetened dried coconut
¼ cup chopped crystallized ginger
¼ cup seedless raisins

Serve slices of this dense, typical Caribbean cross between a cake and a pudding with rum-flavored whipped cream, vanilla custard sauce, or a scoop of coconut ice cream. For the photograph, the plate was dusted with ground cinnamon and garnished with fresh mint and shredded coconut.

Place the sweet potatoes in a pot and add cold water to cover. Bring to a boil over medium-high heat and cook until almost tender, about 35 to 45 minutes. Drain.

As soon as the sweet potatoes are cool enough to handle, peel, cut into chunks, and press through a ricer into a bowl; do not use a food processor as it will make them too smooth.

Preheat an oven to 350° F.

Add the banana, sugar, baking powder, salt, cinnamon, nutmeg, eggs, milk, butter, and rum or vanilla extract to the riced sweet potato. Beat with a wooden spoon or wire whisk until well blended. Fold in the coconut, ginger, and raisins. Pour into a greased 9-by-5-inch loaf pan. Bake until a cake tester comes out clean, about 1½ hours. Transfer to a wire rack to cool for a few minutes, then turn the loaf out onto the rack and cool completely.

Makes 1 loaf, serves 6 to 8.

Index

Recipe Index

ACKNOWLEDGMENTS

To editor Bill LeBlond, who saw the potential in this volume. To copyeditor Sharon Silva for the refinement she brings to my books. And to the rest of the Chronicle Books staff who advise, promote, and distribute my series.

To Burt Tessler at Dishes Delmar, San Francisco, for the loan of vintage ivory-colored dishes.

To Ellen Quan for her invaluable assistance in research, recipe testing, shopping, and food styling.

To Patricia Brabant for yet another sterling achievement in photography, and to her assistant M. J. Murphy for growing potatoes and keeping the studio running.

To Cleve Gallat and Don Kruse at CTA Graphics for another job well done, and for never complaining about last-minute changes.

To my extended family and friends for their consistent support of all my projects.

To Marian May and Louis Hicks for scouring produce markets for perfect potatoes.

To Gregg King and Martin Outzen for their marvelous hospitality and valuable assistance during my prop-shopping spree in New York.

To my sister Martha McNair for her magical assistance in the studio and, along with her husband John Richardson, for looking after my city house while I was writing at Lake Tahoe and prop shopping in New York. And to my nephew Devereux for adding so much pleasure to my life.

To Addie Prey, Buster Booroo, Michael T. Wigglebutt, Joshua J. Chew, and Dweasel Pickle who were on hand throughout the recipe development and writing stages.

And to Lin Cotton for his continual encouragement and his handling of so many business details, thereby freeing me to be more creative.